Casablanca, Morocco Colouring Book

It is well documented that, for many people (adults and children alike), colouring is a therapeutic, stress-relieving pastime.

What could be better, then, than colouring pictures of the vibrant Moroccan city of Casablanca? While away the hours imagining yourself wandering through the streets of the medina, sipping a cocktail in Ricks Café, relaxing on the beach, or admiring the magnificent Hassan II Mosque.

Unlike most other colouring books which are usually filled with whimsical and cartoon images, mine are full of real pictures.

In this case, the colouring pages were created from photographs I took during our month-long tour around Morocco. Within this book, you will find images of mosques, medinas, market stalls, ancient buildings, amazing Art Deco architecture, modern trams, tea sellers in traditional costume, and much more. There are drawings here to inspire you and get your creative juices flowing!!

Grab your favourite pens or pencils and let your imagination and creativity run riot. I use high quality fine-tip felt pens for the details, and coloured pencils for the larger areas, but the choice is yours. Some people like to put a water colour wash across the whole picture before they begin. It's your creation. It's up to you!

Cut out your finished work and display it somewhere as in inspiration to travel further for longer, or as a reminder of places you've already been to.

Keep in touch with me at Happy Days Travel Blog or on social media:

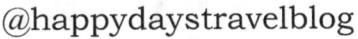

@happydaystravelblog @happydayswriter

Show me your creations, follow my travels, and tell me about yours!

Copyright © 2020 Happy Days Publishing - All Rights Reserved. Further information from https://happydaystravelblog.com

www.ingramcontent.com/pod-product-compliance
Lightning Source LLC
Chambersburg PA
CBHW081655220526
45466CB00009B/2761